ChordBuddy

CHR SONGBOOK

ISBN 978-1-4803-9361-5

HAL•LEONARD®
CORPORATION
7777 W. BLUEMOUND RD. P.O. BOX 13819 MILWAUKEE, WI 53213

Visit Hal Leonard Online at
www.halleonard.com
www.chordbuddy.com

Almost Day

Words and Music by Huddie Ledbetter

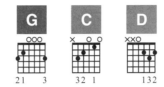

Angels We Have Heard on High

Traditional French Carol
Translated by James Chadwick

Additional Lyrics

2. Shepherds, why this jubilee?
Why your joyous strains prolong?
What the gladsome tidings be
Which inspire your heavenly song?

3. Come to Bethlehem and see
Him whose birth the angels sing.
Come, adore on bended knee
Christ the Lord, the newborn King.

4. See within a manger laid
Jesus, Lord of heaven and earth!
Mary, Joseph, lend your aid,
With us sing our Savior's birth.

As with Gladness Men of Old

Words by William Chatterton Dix
Music by Conrad Kocher

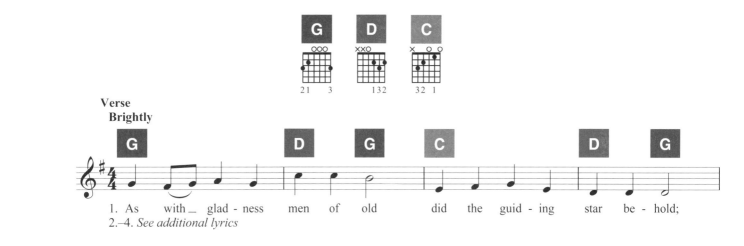

Verse
Brightly

1. As with _ glad - ness men of old did the guid - ing star be - hold;
2.–4. *See additional lyrics*

As with _ joy they hailed its light, lead - ing on - ward, beam - ing bright;

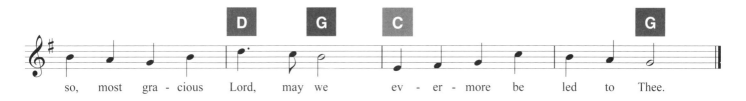

so, most gra - cious Lord, may we ev - er - more be led to Thee.

Additional Lyrics

2. As with joyful steps they sped,
   To that lowly manger bed,
   There to bend the knee before
   Him who Heaven and Earth adore,
   So may we with willing feet
   Ever seek Thy mercy seat.

3. As they offered gifts most rare
   At that manger rude and bare,
   So may we with holy joy,
   Pure and free from sin's alloy,
   All our costliest treasures bring,
   Christ, to Thee, our heavenly King.

4. Holy Jesus, every day
   Keep us in the narrow way;
   And, when earthly things are past,
   Bring our ransomed souls at last
   Where they need no star to guide,
   Where no clouds Thy glory hide.

Away in a Manger

Traditional
Words by John T. McFarland (v.3)
Music by James R. Murray

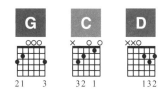

Sweetly

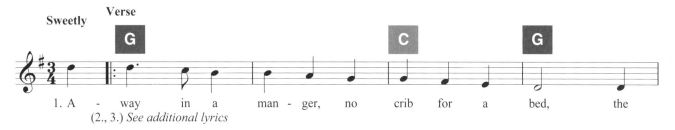

1. A - way in a man - ger, no crib for a bed, the
(2., 3.) *See additional lyrics*

lit - tle Lord Je - sus laid down His sweet head. The

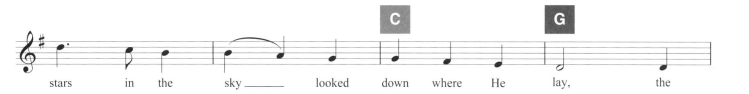

stars in the sky ____ looked down where He lay, the

lit - tle Lord Je - sus, a - sleep on the hay.   2. The there.
                                                   3. Be

Additional Lyrics

2. The cattle are lowing, the Baby awakes,
   But little Lord Jesus, no crying He makes.
   I love Thee, Lord Jesus, look down from the sky
   And stay by my cradle 'til morning is nigh.

3. Be near me, Lord Jesus, I ask Thee to stay
   Close by me forever, and love me, I pray.
   Bless all the dear children in Thy tender care,
   And fit us for heaven to live with Thee there.

Bring a Torch, Jeannette, Isabella

17th Century French Provençal Carol

Additional Lyrics

2. Hasten now, good folk of the village,
   Hasten now, the Christ Child to see.
   You will find him asleep in a manger;
   Quietly come and whisper softly.
   Hush, hush, peacefully now He slumbers.
   Hush, hush, peacefully now He sleeps.

The Chipmunk Song

Words and Music by Ross Bagdasarian

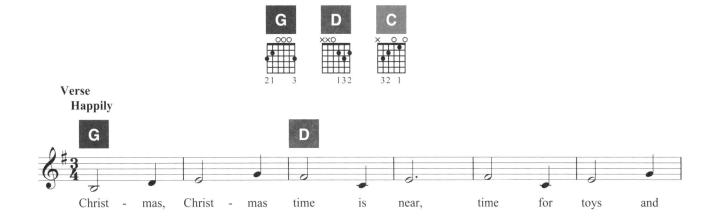

Christ - mas, Christ - mas time is near, time for toys and

time for cheer. We've been good, but we can't last.

Hur - ry, Christ - mas, hur - ry fast! Want a plane that

loops the loop. Me, I want a Hu - la - hoop. We can

hard - ly stand the wait. Please, Christ - mas, don't be late. _____

Child of God

Words and Music by Grant Cunningham and Matt Huesmann

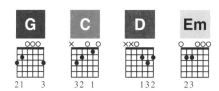

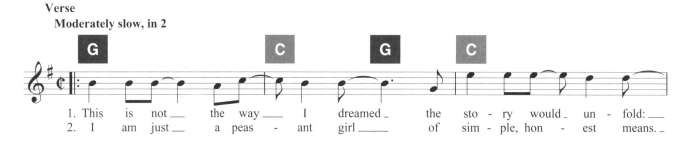

Verse
Moderately slow, in 2

1. This is not ___ the way ___ I dreamed ___ the sto - ry would ___ un - fold: ___
2. I am just ___ a peas - ant girl ___ of sim - ple, hon - est means. ___

___ a sta - ble and ___ a bed ___ of hay, ___ a
___ Who am I ___ to hold ___ the Sav - ior

night so clear ___ and cold. ___ The on - ly Child ___ of God ___
sent to set ___ men free, ___ to know the Child ___ that I ___

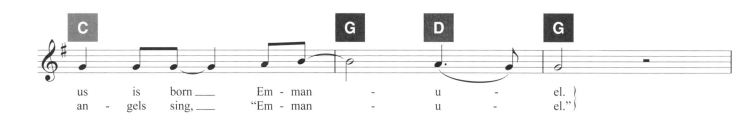

___ be - got - ten, in my arms ___ I hold. ___ To
___ gave life ___ will in give His life ___ for me? ___ The

us is born ___ Em - man - u - el. }
an - gels sing, ___ "Em - man - u - el." }

Christmas Is A-Comin'
(May God Bless You)

Words and Music by Frank Luther

Come, Thou Long-Expected Jesus

Words by Charles Wesley
Music by Rowland Hugh Prichard

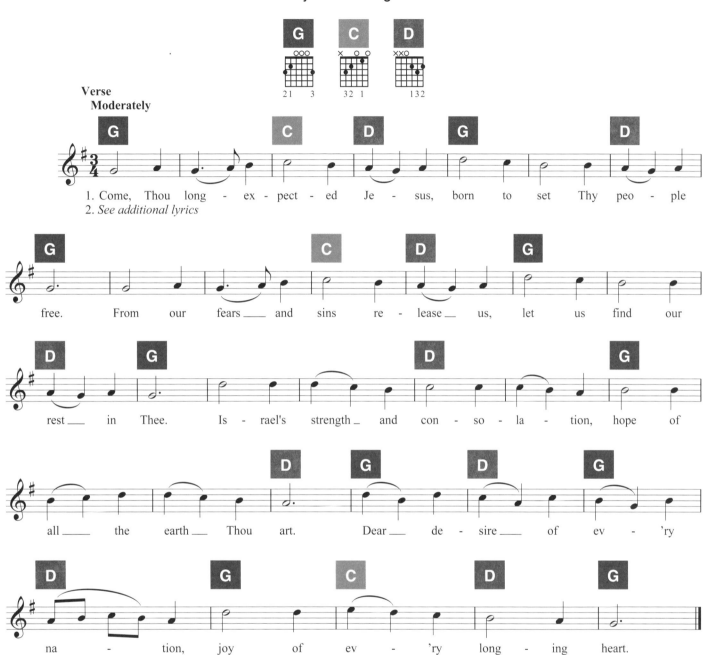

Verse
Moderately

1. Come, Thou long - ex - pect - ed Je - sus, born to set Thy peo - ple
2. *See additional lyrics*

free. From our fears ___ and sins re - lease ___ us, let us find our

rest ___ in Thee. Is - rael's strength ___ and con - so - la - tion, hope of

all ___ the earth ___ Thou art. Dear ___ de - sire ___ of ev - 'ry

na - tion, joy of ev - 'ry long - ing heart.

Additional Lyrics

2. Born Thy people to deliver,
   Born a child and yet a King.
   Born to reign in us forever,
   Now Thy gracious kingdom bring.
   By Thine own eternal Spirit,
   Rule in all our hearts alone.
   By Thine all sufficient merit,
   Raise us to Thy glorious throne.

Deck the Hall

Traditional Welsh Carol

Verse
Brightly, in 2

1. Deck the hall with boughs of hol-ly; fa, la, la, la, la, la, la, la, la.
2., 3. *See additional lyrics*

'Tis the sea-son to be jol-ly; fa, la, la, la, la, la, la, la, la.

Don we now our gay ap-par-el; fa, la, la, la, la, la, la, la, la.

Troll the an-cient yule-tide car-ol; fa, la, la, la, la, la, la, la, la.

Additional Lyrics

2. See the blazing yule before us;
   Fa, la, la, la, la, la, la, la, la.
   Strike the harp and join the chorus;
   Fa, la, la, la, la, la, la, la, la.
   Follow me in merry measure;
   Fa, la, la, la, la, la, la, la, la.
   While I tell of Yuletide treasure;
   Fa, la, la, la, la, la, la, la, la.

3. Fast away the old year passes;
   Fa, la, la, la, la, la, la, la, la.
   Hail the new, ye lads and lasses;
   Fa, la, la, la, la, la, la, la, la.
   Sing we joyous all together;
   Fa, la, la, la, la, la, la, la, la.
   Heedless of the wind and weather;
   Fa, la, la, la, la, la, la, la, la.

Ding Dong! Merrily on High!

French Carol

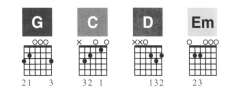

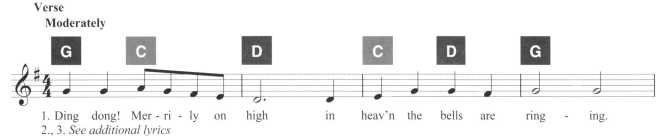

Verse
Moderately

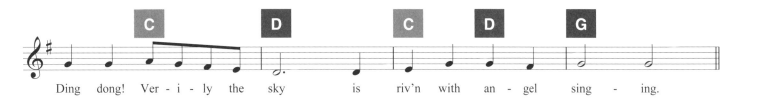

1. Ding dong! Mer - ri - ly on high in heav'n the bells are ring - ing.
2., 3. *See additional lyrics*

Ding dong! Ver - i - ly the sky is riv'n with an - gel sing - ing.

Chorus

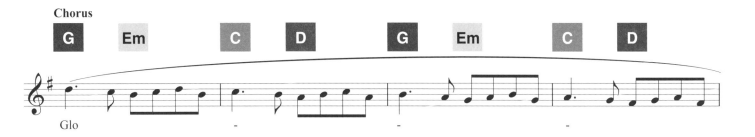

Glo - - - - -

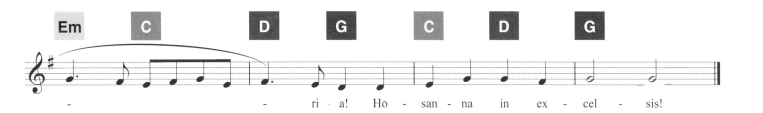

- - ri - a! Ho - san - na in ex - cel - sis!

Additional Lyrics

2. E'en so here below, below, let steeple bells be swinging.
   And i-o, i-o, i-o, by priest and people singing.

3. Pray you, dutifully prime your matin chime, ye ringers.
   May you beautiful rime your evetime song, ye singers.

Emmanuel
(Hallowed Manger Ground)

Words and Music by Chris Tomlin and Ed Cash

17

Feliz Navidad

Music and Lyrics by José Feliciano

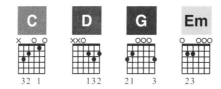

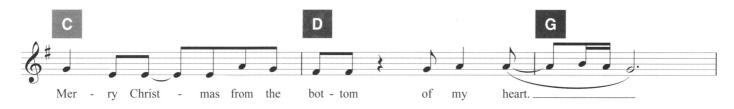

The First Noel

17th Century English Carol
Music from W. Sandys' *Christmas Carols*

Additional Lyrics

2. They looked up and saw a star
   Shining in the east, beyond them far.
   And to the earth it gave great light
   And so it continued both day and night.

3. And by the light of that same star,
   Three wise men came from country far;
   To seek for a King was their intent,
   And to follow the star wherever it went.

4. This star drew nigh to the northwest,
   O'er Bethlehem it took its rest;
   And there it did both stop and stay,
   Right over the place where Jesus lay.

5. Then entered in those wise men three,
   Full reverently upon their knee;
   And offered there in His presence,
   Their gold, and myrrh, and frankincense.

The Friendly Beasts

Traditional English Carol

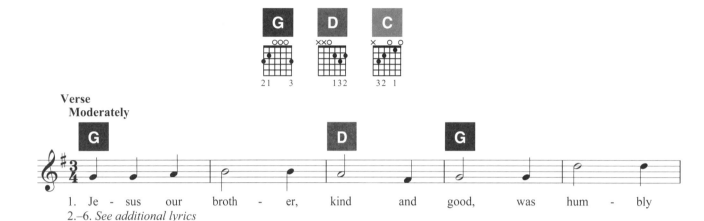

Verse
Moderately

1. Je - sus our broth - er, kind and good, was hum - bly
2.–6. *See additional lyrics*

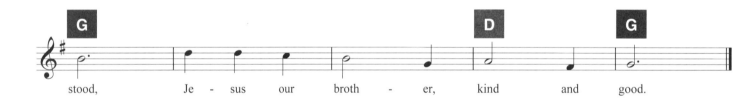

born in a sta - ble rude; and the friend - ly beasts a - round Him

stood, Je - sus our broth - er, kind and good.

Additional Lyrics

2. "I," said the donkey, shaggy and brown,
   "I carried His mother up hill and down.
   I carried His mother to Bethlehem town."
   "I," said the donkey, shaggy and brown.

3. "I," said the cow, all white and red,
   "I gave him my manger for His bed.
   I gave Him my hay to pillow His head."
   "I," said the cow, all white and red.

4. "I," said the sheep with the curly horn,
   "I gave Him my wool for His blanket warm.
   He wore my coat on Christmas morn."
   "I," said the sheep with the curly horn.

5. "I," said the dove from the rafters high,
   "I cooed Him to sleep that He would not cry.
   We cooed Him to sleep, my mate and I."
   "I," said the dove from the rafters high.

6. Thus every beast by some good spell,
   In the stable dark was glad to tell
   Of the gift he gave Emmanuel,
   The gift he gave Emmanuel.

Glad Tidings
(Shalom Chaverim)

English Lyrics and New Music Arranged by Ronnie Gilbert, Lee Hays, Fred Hellerman and Pete Seeger

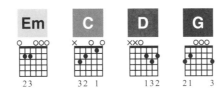

Frosty the Snow Man

Words and Music by Steve Nelson and Jack Rollins

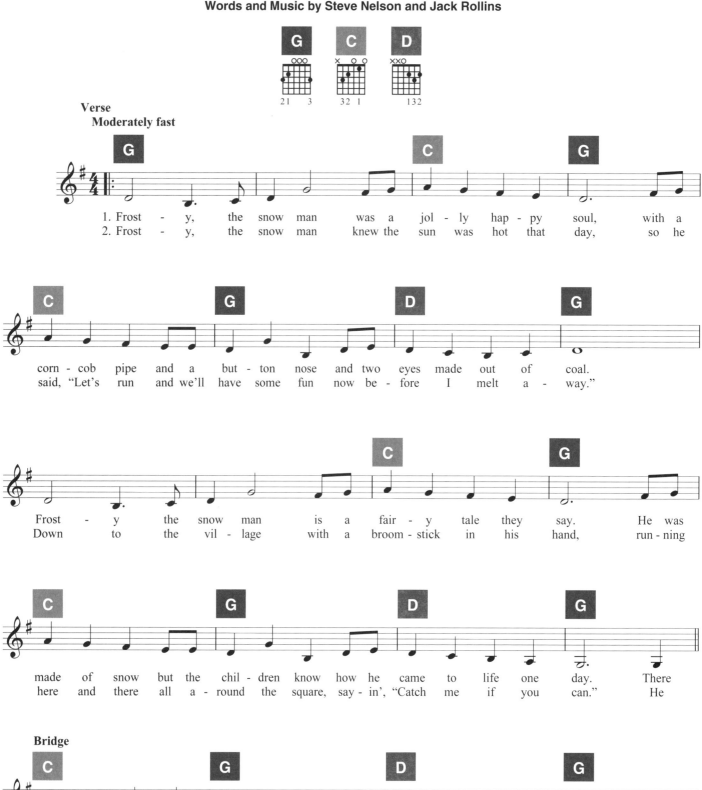

when they placed it on his head he be - gan to dance a - round. Oh,
on - ly paused a mo - ment when __ he heard him hol - ler, "Stop!" For

Verse

Frost - y the snow man was a - live as he could be, and the
Frost - y the snow man had to hur - ry on his way, but he

chil - dren say he could laugh and play just the same as you and me.
waved good - bye say - in', "Don't you cry, I'll be back a - gain some day."

Outro

Thump-et - y thump thump, thump-et - y thump thump, look at Frost - y go.

Thump-et - y thump thump, thump-et - y thump thump, o - ver the hills of snow.

Go, Tell It on the Mountain

African-American Spiritual
Verses by John W. Work, Jr.

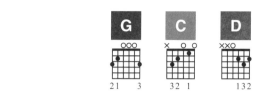

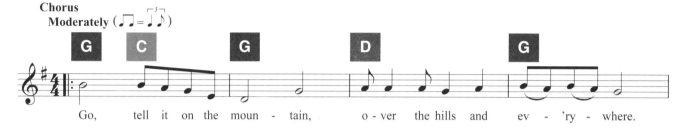

Go, tell it on the moun - tain, o - ver the hills and ev - 'ry - where.

Go, tell it on the moun - tain, that Je - sus Christ is born. 1. While shep - herds kept their
2., 3. *See additional lyrics*

watch - ing o'er si - lent flocks by night, be - hold, through - out the

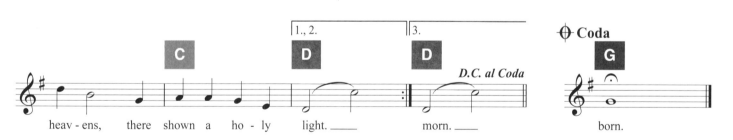

heav - ens, there shown a ho - ly light. morn. born.

Additional Lyrics

2. The shepherds feared and trembled
   When, lo! above the earth
   Rang out the angel chorus
   That hailed our Savior's birth.

3. Down in a lowly manger
   Our humble Christ was born.
   And God sent us salvation
   That blessed Christmas morn.

Good Christian Men, Rejoice

14th Century Latin Text
Translated by John Mason Neale
14th Century German Melody

Verse
With spirit

1. Good Chris - tian men, re - joice _____ with heart and soul and voice. _____
2., 3. *See additional lyrics*

Give ye heed to what we say: News! News! Je - sus Christ is born to - day!

Ox and ass be - fore Him bow, and He is in the man - ger now.

Christ is born to - day! _____ Christ is born to - day!

Additional Lyrics

2. Good Christian men, rejoice
   With heart and soul and voice.
   Now ye hear of endless bliss: Joy! Joy!
   Jesus Christ was born for this!
   He hath op'd the heavenly door,
   And man is blessed evermore.
   Christ was born for this!
   Christ was born for this!

3. Good Christian men, rejoice
   With heart and soul and voice.
   Now ye need not fear the grave: Peace! Peace!
   Jesus Christ was born to save!
   Calls you one and calls you all
   To gain His everlasting hall.
   Christ was born to save!
   Christ was born to save!

Good King Wenceslas

Words by John M. Neale
Music from *Piae Cantiones*

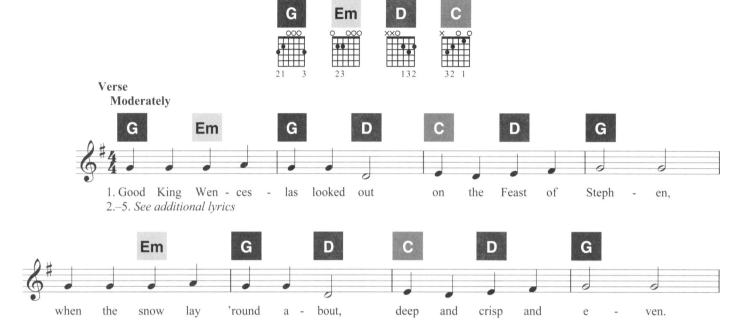

1. Good King Wen - ces - las looked out on the Feast of Steph - en,
2.–5. *See additional lyrics*

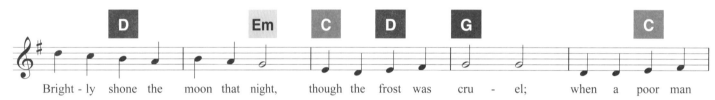

when the snow lay 'round a - bout, deep and crisp and e - ven.

Bright - ly shone the moon that night, though the frost was cru - el; when a poor man

came in sight, gath - 'ring win - ter fu - el.

Additional Lyrics

2. "Hither page, and stand by me,
If thou know'st it telling;
Yonder peasant, who is he?
Where and what his dwelling?"
"Sire, he lives a good league hence,
Underneath the mountain;
Right against the forest fence,
By Saint Agnes' fountain."

3. "Bring me flesh, and bring me wine,
Bring me pine logs hither;
Thou and I will see him dine,
When we bear then thither."
Page and monarch forth they went,
Forth they went together;
Through the rude wind's wild lament,
And the bitter weather.

4. "Sire, the night is darker now,
And the wind blows stronger;
Fails my heart, I know not how.
I can go no longer."
"Mark my footsteps, my good page,
Tread thou in them boldly;
Thou shalt find the winter's rage
Freeze thy blood less coldly."

5. In his master's steps he trod,
Where the snow lay dinted;
Heat was in the very sod
Which the saint has printed.
Therefore, Christian men, be sure,
Wealth or rank possessing;
Ye who now will bless the poor,
Shall yourselves find blessing.

Grandma Got Run Over by a Reindeer

Words and Music by Randy Brooks

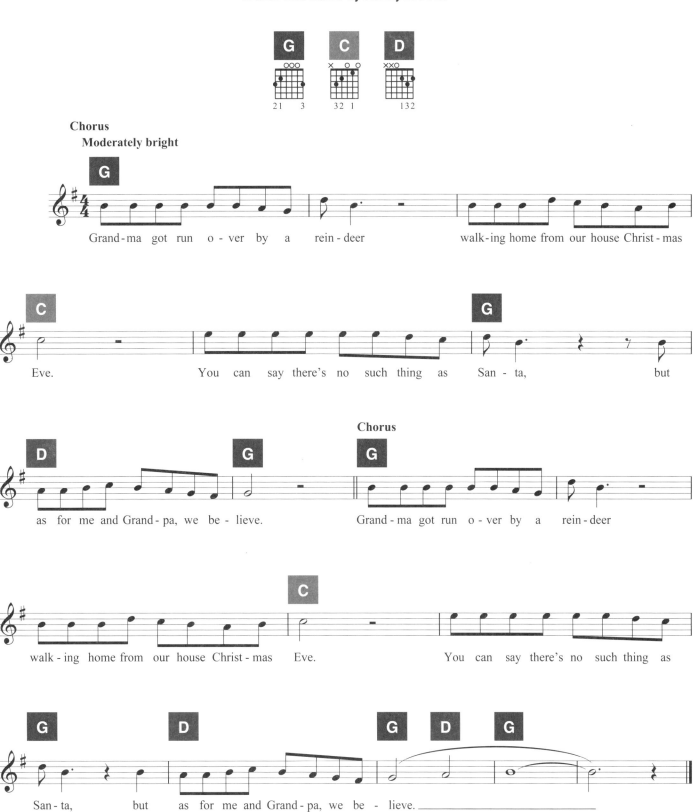

Grandma's Killer Fruitcake

Words and Music by Elmo Shropshire and Rita Abrams

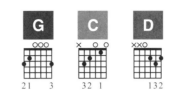

Verse
Country Polka, in 2

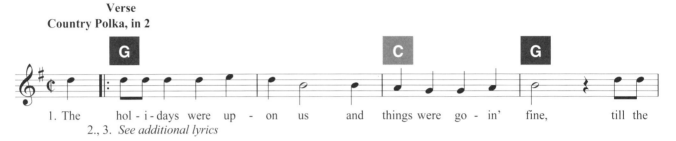

1. The hol-i-days were up-on us and things were go-in' fine, till the
2., 3. *See additional lyrics*

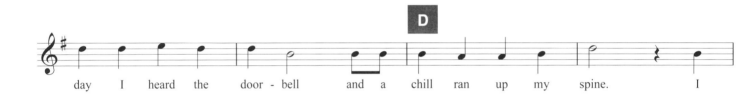

day I heard the door-bell and a chill ran up my spine. I

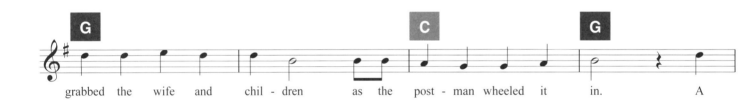

grabbed the wife and chil-dren as the post-man wheeled it in. A

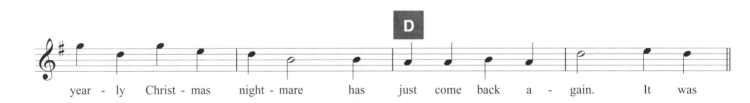

year-ly Christ-mas night-mare has just come back a-gain. It was

Chorus

hard-er than the head of Un-cle Buck-y, heav-y as a ser-mon of

Preach - er Luck - y. One's e - nough to give the whole state of Ken - tuck - y a

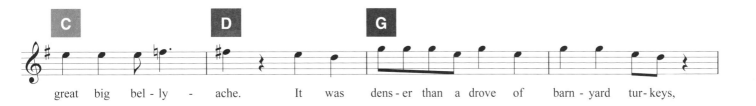

great big bel - ly - ache. It was dens - er than a drove of barn - yard tur - keys,

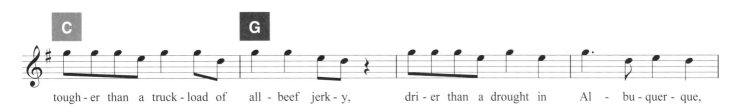

tough - er than a truck - load of all - beef jerk - y, dri - er than a drought in Al - bu - quer - que,

Grand - ma's kill - er fruit - cake. cake. _____

Additional Lyrics

2. Now, I've had to swallow some marginal fare at our family feast.
   I even downed Aunt Dolly's possom pie just to keep the family peace.
   I winced at Wilma's gizzard mousse, but said it tasted fine.
   But that lethal weapon that Grandma bakes is where I draw the line.

3. It's early Christmas morning, the phone rings us awake.
   It's Grandma, Pa, she wants to know how'd we like the cake.
   "Well, Grandma, I never. Uh, we couldn't. It was, uh, unbelievable, that's for sure!
   What's that you say? Oh, no, Grandma. Puh-leez don't send us anymore!"

Hark! The Herald Angels Sing

Words by Charles Wesley
Music by Felix Mendelssohn-Bartholdy

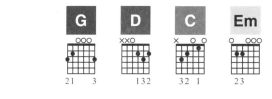

Verse
Joyfully

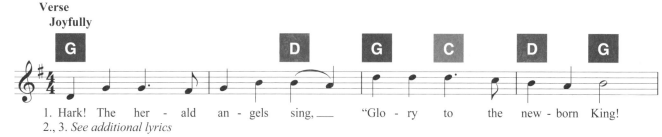

1. Hark! The her - ald an - gels sing, ___ "Glo - ry to the new - born King!
2., 3. *See additional lyrics*

Peace on earth, and mer - cy mild, ___ God and sin - ners re - con - ciled."

Joy - ful all ye na - tions rise. ___ Join the tri - umph of the skies. ___

With th'an - gel - ic host pro - claim, "Christ is ___ born in Beth - le - hem."

Hark! The her - ald an - gels sing, "Glo - ry ___ to the new - born King!"

Additional Lyrics

2. Christ, by highest heav'n adored,
   Christ, the everlasting Lord;
   Late in time behold Him come,
   Offspring of the Virgin's womb.
   Veil'd in flesh the Godhead see:
   Hail th'Incarnate Deity.
   Pleased as Man with man to dwell,
   Jesus, our Emmanuel!
   Hark! The herald angels sing,
   "Glory to the newborn King!"

3. Hail, the heav'n-born Prince of Peace!
   Hail the Son of Righteousness!
   Light and life to all He brings,
   Ris'n with healing in His wings.
   Mild, He lays his glory by,
   Born that man no more may die;
   Born to raise the sons of earth,
   Born to give them second birth.
   Hark! The herald angels sing,
   "Glory to the newborn King!"

He Is Born, the Holy Child
(Il Est Ne, Le Divin Enfant)

Traditional French Carol

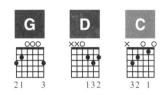

Chorus
Moderately, in 2

He is born, the ___ Ho-ly Child. Play the ___ o-boe and

bag-pipes mer-ri-ly. He is born, the ___ Ho-ly Child. Sing we all of the

Sav-ior's birth. 1. Through long a-ges ___ of the past,
2., 3. *See additional lyrics*

Fine **Verse**

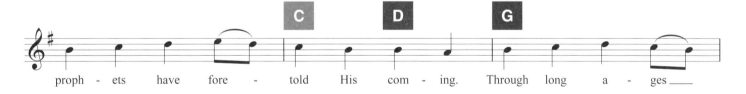

proph-ets have fore-told His com-ing. Through long a-ges ___

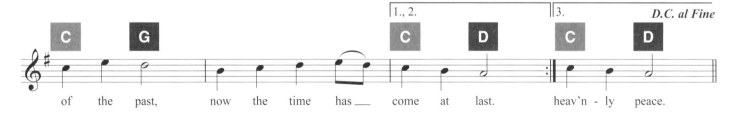

of the past, now the time has ___ come at last. heav'n-ly peace.

Additional Lyrics

2. Oh, how lovely, oh, how pure,
   Is this perfect Child of heaven.
   Oh, how lovely, oh, how pure,
   Gracious gift of God to man.

3. Jesus, Lord of all the world,
   Coming as a Child among us.
   Jesus, Lord of all the world,
   Grant to us Thy heav'nly peace.

Here Comes Santa Claus
(Right Down Santa Claus Lane)

Words and Music by Gene Autry and Oakley Haldeman

Verse
Moderately, in 2

1. Here comes San-ta Claus! Here comes San-ta Claus! Right down San-ta Claus Lane!
2.–4. *See additional lyrics*

Vix-en and Blitz-en and all his rein-deer are pull-ing on the rein. Bells are ring-ing, chil-dren sing-ing, all is mer-ry and bright. Hang your stock-ings and say your prayers, 'cause San-ta Claus comes to-night. night.

Additional Lyrics

2. Here comes Santa Claus! Here comes Santa Claus!
Right down Santa Claus Lane!
He's got a bag that is filled with toys
For the boys and girls again.
Hear those sleigh bells jingle, jangle,
What a beautiful sight.
Jump in bed, cover up your head,
'Cause Santa Claus comes tonight.

3. Here comes Santa Claus! Here comes Santa Claus!
Right down Santa Claus Lane!
He doesn't care if you're rich or poor,
For he loves you just the same.
Santa knows that we're God's children;
That makes ev'rything right.
Fill your hearts with a Christmas cheer,
'Cause Santa Claus comes tonight.

4. Here comes Santa Claus! Here comes Santa Claus!
Right down Santa Claus Lane!
He'll come around when the chimes ring out;
Then it's Christmas morn again.
Peace on earth will come to all
If we just follow the light.
Let's give thanks to the Lord above,
'Cause Santa Claus comes tonight.

Here We Come A-Wassailing

Traditional

The Holly and the Ivy

18th Century English Carol

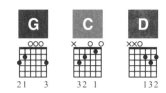

Verse
Moderately slow

1. The hol - ly and the i - vy, when they are both full grown, of ___
2.–5. *See additional lyrics*

all the trees that are in the wood, the ___ hol - ly bears the crown. The

Chorus

ris - ing of the sun ___ and the run - ning of the deer. The ___

play - ing of the mer - ry or - gan, sweet sing - ing of the choir.

Additional Lyrics

2. The holly bears a blossom,
   As white as lily flow'r,
   And Mary bore sweet Jesus Christ,
   To be our sweet Saviour.

3. The holly bears a berry,
   As red as any blood,
   And Mary bore sweet Jesus Christ,
   To do poor sinners good.

4. The holly bears a prickle,
   As sharp as any thorn,
   And Mary bore sweet Jesus Christ,
   On Christmas Day in the morn.

5. The holly bears a bark,
   As bitter as any gall,
   And Mary bore sweet Jesus Christ,
   For to redeem us all.

A Holly Jolly Christmas

Music and Lyrics by Johnny Marks

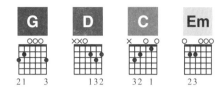

I Heard the Bells on Christmas Day

Words by Henry Wadsworth Longfellow
Music by John Baptiste Calkin

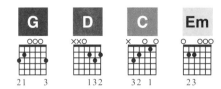

Verse
Moderately slow

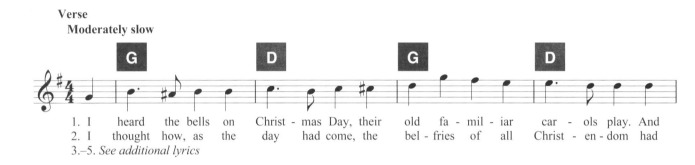

1. I heard the bells on Christ - mas Day, their old fa - mil - iar car - ols play. And
2. I thought how, as the day had come, the bel - fries of all Christ - en - dom had
3.–5. *See additional lyrics*

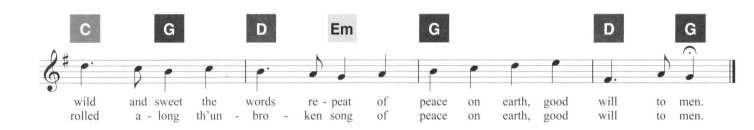

wild and sweet the words re - peat of peace on earth, good will to men.
rolled a - long th'un - bro - ken song of peace on earth, good will to men.

Additional Lyrics

3. And in despair I bowed my head:
   "There is no peace on earth," I said.
   "For hate is strong, and mocks the song
   Of peace on earth, good will to men."

4. Then pealed the bells more loud and deep:
   "God is not dead, nor doth He sleep.
   The wrong shall fail, the right prevail
   With peace on earth, good will to men."

5. Till, ringing, singing on its way,
   The world revolved from night to day.
   A voice, a chime, a chant sublime,
   Of peace on earth, good will to men.

I Saw Three Ships

Traditional English Carol

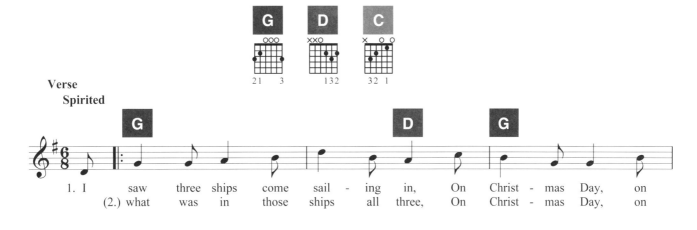

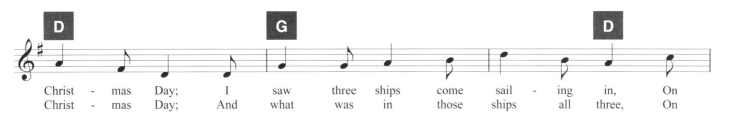

1. I saw three ships come sail - ing in, On Christ - mas Day, on
(2.) what was in those ships all three, On Christ - mas Day, on

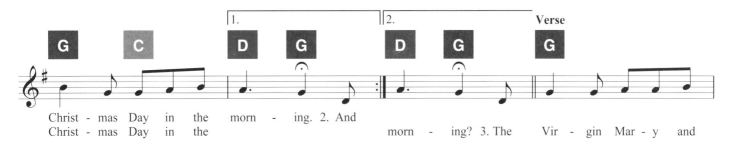

Christ - mas Day; I saw three ships come sail - ing in, On
Christ - mas Day; And saw what was in those ships all three, On

Christ - mas Day in the morn - ing. 2. And
Christ - mas Day in the   morn - ing? 3. The Vir - gin Mar - y and

Christ were there, On Christ - mas Day, on Christ - mas Day; The

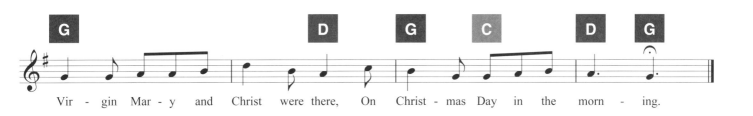

Vir - gin Mar - y and Christ were there, On Christ - mas Day in the morn - ing.

I'll Be Home on Christmas Day

Words and Music by Michael Jarrett

Verse
Moderately slow, in 2

1. From the hills of Geor - gia, a - cross the
2. It's been so man - y _____ times be - fore she left that
3. There were times I'd think a - bout _____ her, all the love

plains _____ of Ten - nes - see, _____ I've
can - dle burn - ing. And
I _____ left be - hind. And

seen and I've done _____ most ev - 'ry - thing that a
all too _____ man - y tears that fell, my
mem - o - ries _____ still lin - ger with -

man can _____ do or see. But if I _____
soul _____ filled with yearn - ing If I had _____
in my _____ trou - bled mind. If I could _____

_____ could on - ly bor - row one dream _____ from yes - ter -
_____ an - y sense at all, I'd just be _____ on my
_____ set a - side my pride, then I'd be _____ on my

day,
way.
way.
I'd be on that train to - mor - row.
I'd be on that train to - mor - row.
I'd catch that train to - mor - row.

I'll be home on Christ - mas day.

1., 2.

3.   **Outro**

If I had an - y sense at all, I'd just

be on my way. I'd catch that train

1.

to - mor - row. I'll be home on Christ - mas

2.

day. I said, I'll home on Christ - mas day.

Infant Holy, Infant Lowly

Traditional Polish Carol
Paraphrased by Edith M.G. Reed

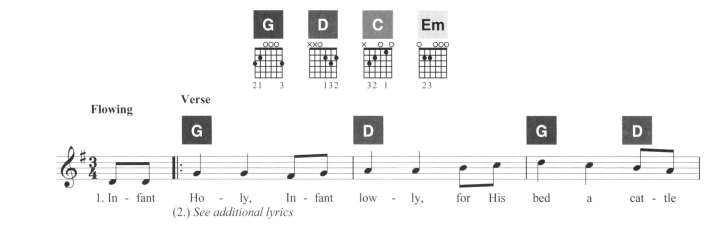

Flowing

Verse

1. In-fant Ho-ly, In-fant low-ly, for His bed a cat-tle
(2.) *See additional lyrics*

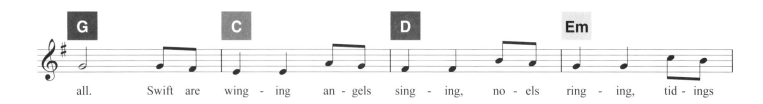

stall. Ox-en low-ing, lit-tle know-ing Christ the Babe is Lord of

all. Swift are wing-ing an-gels sing-ing, no-els ring-ing, tid-ings

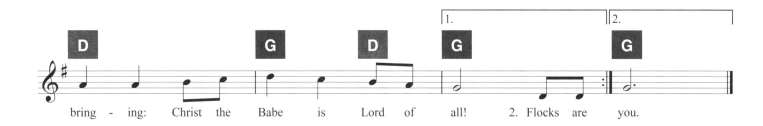

bring-ing: Christ the Babe is Lord of all! 2. Flocks are you.

Additional Lyrics

2. Flocks are sleeping, shepherds keeping
   Vigil 'til the morning new.
   Saw the glory, heard the story,
   Tidings of a Gospel true.
   Thus rejoicing, free from sorrow,
   Praises voicing, greet the morrow.
   Christ the Babe was born for you.

Jingle Bells

Words and Music by J. Pierpont

Additional Lyrics

2. A day or two ago, I thought I'd take a ride,
And soon Miss Fannie Bright was sitting by my side.
The horse was lean and lank, misfortune seemed his lot.
He got into a drifted bank and we, we got upsot! Oh!

3. Now the ground is white, go it while you're young.
Take the girls tonight and sing this sleighing song.
Just get a bobtail bay, two-forty for his speed.
Then hitch him to an open sleigh and crack, you'll take the lead! Oh!

It Won't Seem Like Christmas
(Without You)

Words and Music by J.A. Balthrop

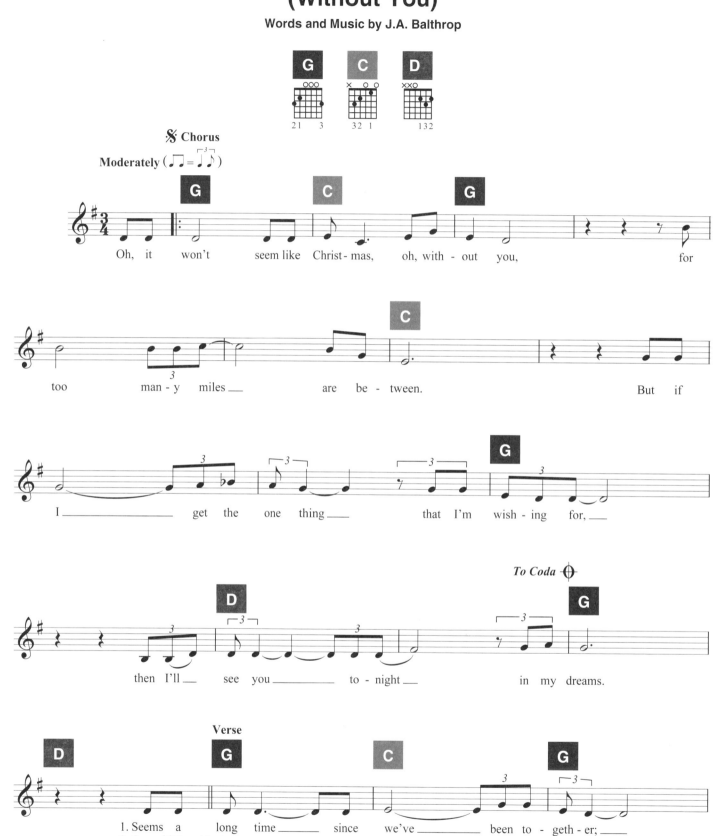

it was just a-bout _____ to this time of year. _____

Looks like it's _____ gon-na be _____ snow-y weath-er. _____

How I wish that you could be here. _____

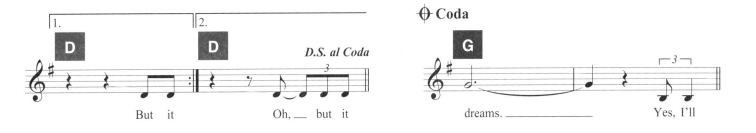

1.
But it

2.
D.S. al Coda
Oh, ___ but it

✛ **Coda**

dreams. _____ Yes, I'll

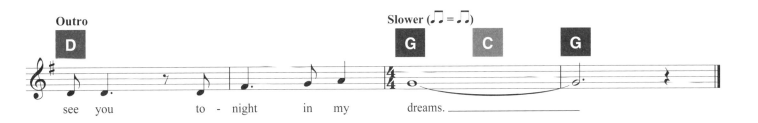

Outro

see you to-night in my dreams. _____

Additional Lyrics

2. In the distance I hear sleigh bells ringing.
   The holly's so pretty this year;
   And the carol that somebody's singing
   Reminds me of our Christmas last year.

Jolly Old St. Nicholas

Traditional 19th Century American Carol

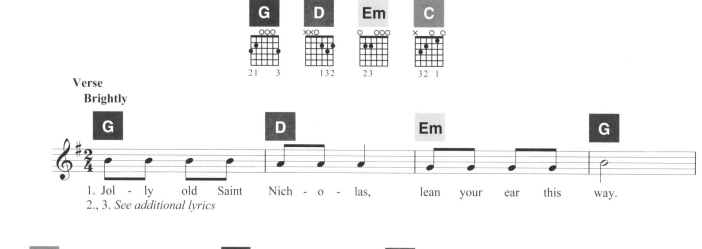

Verse
Brightly

1. Jol - ly old Saint Nich - o - las, lean your ear this way.
2., 3. *See additional lyrics*

Don't you tell a sin - gle soul what I'm going to say.

Christ - mas Eve is com - ing soon; now, you dear old man,

whis - per what you'll bring to me. Tell me if you can.

Additional Lyrics

2. When the clock is striking twelve, when I'm fast asleep,
   Down the chimney broad and black, with your pack you'll creep.
   All the stockings you will find hanging in a row.
   Mine will be the shortest one; you'll be sure to know.

3. Johnny wants a pair of skates, Susy wants a sled.
   Nellie wants a picture book: yellow, blue and red.
   Now I think I'll leave to you what to give the rest.
   Choose for me, dear Santa Claus; you will know the best.

Joy to the World

Words by Isaac Watts
Music by George Frideric Handel
Adapted by Lowell Mason

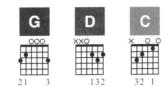

Verse
With spirit

1. Joy to the world! The Lord is come: Let earth re-
2.–4. *See additional lyrics*

ceive her King. Let ev-'ry ____ heart ____ pre-pare ____ Him ____

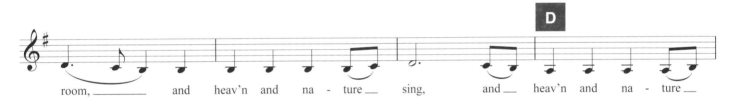

room, ____ and heav'n and na-ture ____ sing, and ____ heav'n and na-ture ____

sing, and ____ heav'n ____ and heav'n ____ and na-ture sing.

Additional Lyrics

2. Joy to the earth! The Savior reigns;
Let men their songs employ
While fields and floods, rocks, hills and plains
Repeat the sounding joy,
Repeat the sounding joy,
Repeat, repeat the sounding joy.

3. No more let sin and sorrow grow,
Nor thorns infest the ground.
He comes to make His blessings flow
Far as the curse is found,
Far as the curse is found,
Far as, far as the curse is found.

4. He rules the world with truth and grace
And makes the nations prove
The glories of His righteousness,
And wonders of His love,
And wonders of His love,
And wonders, wonders of His love.

The Little Drummer Boy

Words and Music by Harry Simeone, Henry Onorati and Katherine Davis

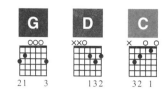

Verse
Moderately slow, in 2

1. Come, they told me, pa rum pum pum pum, ____
2. Ba - by Je - su, pa rum pum pum pum, ____
3. Mar - y nod - ded, pa rum pum pum pum. ____

____ our new - born King to see, pa
____ I am a poor boy, too, pa
____ The ox and lamb kept time, pa

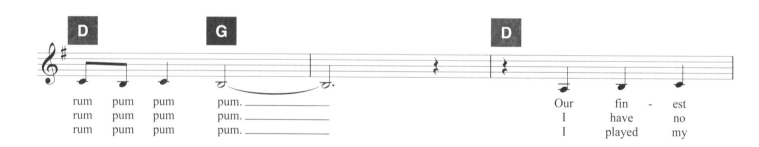

rum pum pum pum. ____ Our fin - est
rum pum pum pum. ____ I have no
rum pum pum pum. ____ I played my

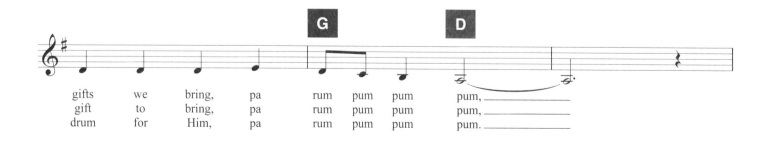

gifts we bring, pa rum pum pum pum, ____
gift to bring, pa rum pum pum pum, ____
drum for Him, pa rum pum pum pum. ____

to lay be - fore the King, pa rum pum pum pum,
that's fit to give our King, pa rum pum pum pum,
I played my best for Him, pa rum pum pum pum,

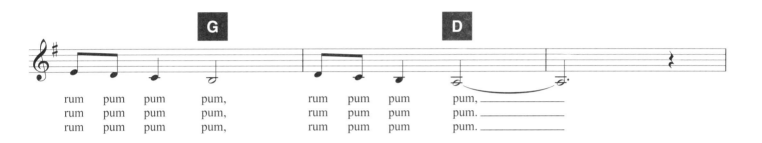

rum pum pum pum, rum pum pum pum, _____
rum pum pum pum, rum pum pum pum. _____
rum pum pum pum, rum pum pum pum. _____

so to hon - or Him, pa rum pum pum pum, _____
Shall I play for you, pa rum pum pum pum, _____
Then He smiled at me, pa rum pum pum pum, _____

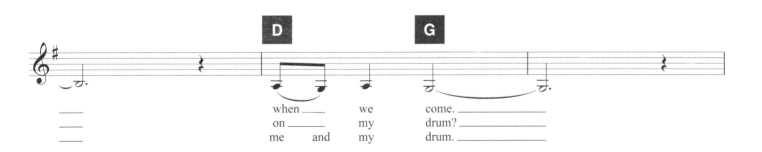

____ when ____ we come.
____ on ____ my drum?
____ me and my drum.

1., 2.   3.

Mary Had a Baby

African-American Spiritual

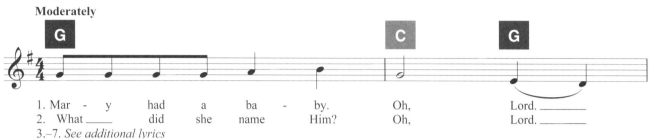

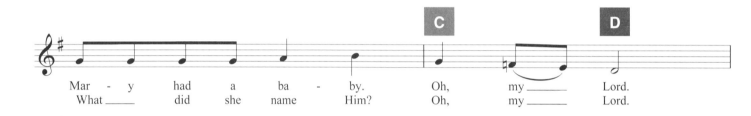

1. Mar - y had a ba - by. Oh, Lord. _____
2. What _____ did she name Him? Oh, Lord. _____
3.–7. *See additional lyrics*

Mar - y had a ba - by. Oh, my _____ Lord.
What _____ did she name Him? Oh, my _____ Lord.

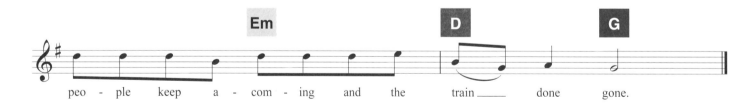

Mar - y had a ba - by. ⎫
What _____ did she name Him? ⎬ Oh, Lord. _____ The

peo - ple keep a - com - ing and the train _____ done gone.

Additional Lyrics

3. She called Him Jesus.
4. Where was He born?
5. Born in a stable.
6. Where did they lay Him?
7. Laid Him in a manger.

Mary's Little Boy

Words and Music by Massie Patterson and Sammy Heyward

Additional Lyrics

2. Soldiers looked for the little boy,
   Soldiers looked for the little boy,
   Soldiers looked for the little boy,
   And they said His name was Wonderful.

3. Wise men came running from the East,
   Wise men came running from the East,
   Wise men came running from the East,
   And they said His name was Wonderful.

Merry Christmas, Baby

Words and Music by Lou Baxter and Johnny Moore

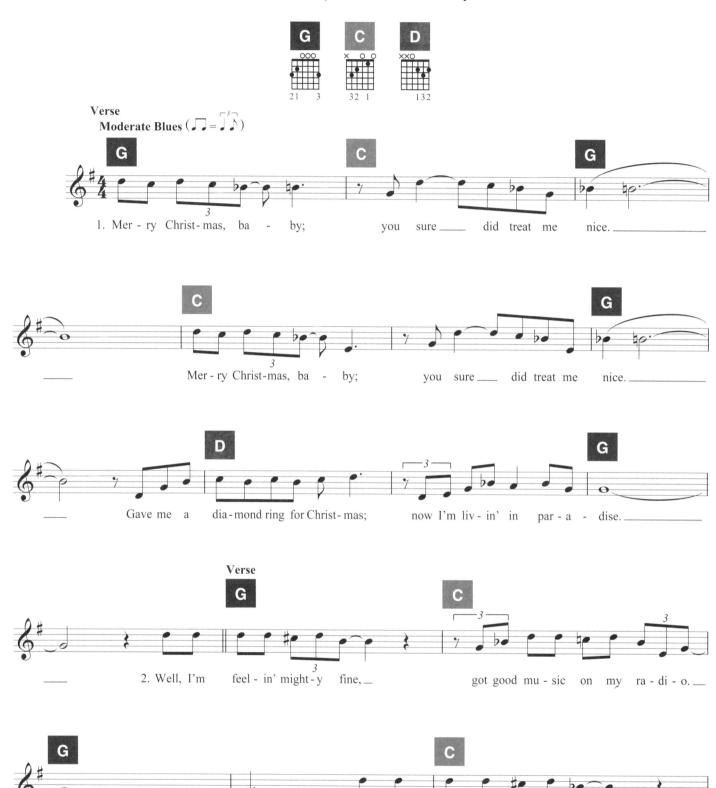

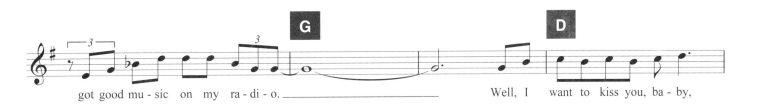

got good mu - sic on my ra - di - o. _____ Well, I want to kiss you, ba - by,

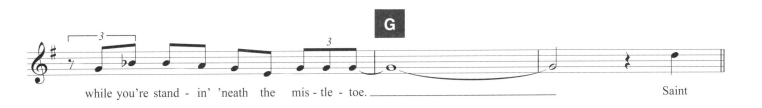

while you're stand - in' 'neath the mis - tle - toe. _____ Saint

Outro-Verse

Nick came down the chim - ney 'bout half - past three, ___ left all these pret - ty pres - ents ___ that you

see be - fore me. ___ Mer - ry Christ - mas, lit - tle ba - by; you sure ___ been good to

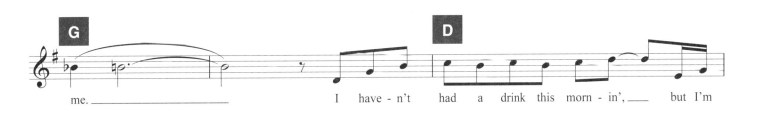

me. _____ I have - n't had a drink this morn - in', ___ but I'm

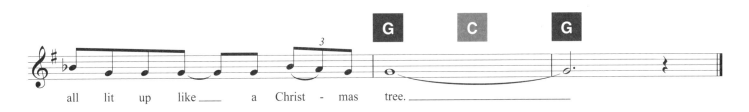

all lit up like ___ a Christ - mas tree. _____

Merry Christmas from the Family

Words and Music by Robert Earl Keen

Additional Lyrics

3. Fran and Rita drove from Harlingen; I can't remember how I'm kin to them.
But when they tried to plug their motor home in, they blew our Christmas lights.
Cousin David knew just what went wrong, so we all waited out on our front lawn.
He threw the breaker and the lights came on and we sang, "Silent night, oh, silent night."

A Merry, Merry Christmas to You

Music and Lyrics by Johnny Marks

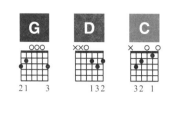

Chorus
Spirited, in 1

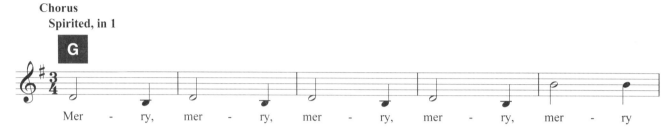

Mer - ry, mer - ry, mer - ry, mer - ry, mer - ry

Christ - mas to you. _____ May each day be ver - y,

ver - y hap - py all the year through. _____ A -

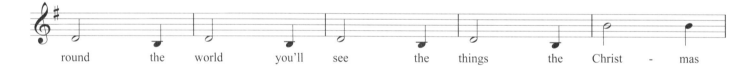

round the world you'll see the things the Christ - mas

spir - it can do. _____ Bells will be ring - ing with

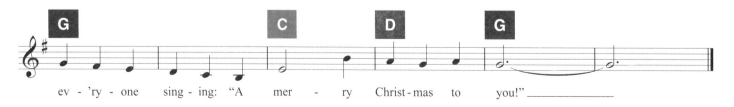

ev - 'ry - one sing - ing: "A mer - ry Christ - mas to you!" _____

O Christmas Tree

Traditional German Carol

Verse
Moderately

1. O, Christ - mas tree, O Christ - mas tree, you stand in ver - dant beau - ty! O
(2., 3.) *See additional lyrics*

Christ - mas tree, O Christ - mas tree, you stand in ver - dant beau - ty! Your

boughs are green in sum - mer's glow, and do not fade in win - ter's snow. O

Christ - mas tree, O Christ - mas tree, you stand in ver - dant beau - ty! 2., 3. O bright - ly.

Additional Lyrics

2. O Christmas tree, O Christmas tree,
Much pleasure doth thou bring me!
O Christmas tree, O Christmas tree,
Much pleasure doth thou bring me!
For every year the Christmas tree
Brings to us all both joy and glee.
O Christmas tree, O Christmas tree,
Much pleasure doth thou bring me!

3. O Christmas tree, O Christmas tree,
Thy candles shine out brightly!
O Christmas tree, O Christmas tree,
Thy candles shine out brightly!
Each bough doth hold its tiny light
That makes each toy to sparkle bright.
O Christmas tree, O Christmas tree,
Thy candles shine out brightly.

Mistletoe

Words and Music by Justin Bieber, Nasri Atweh and Adam Messinger

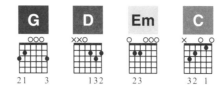

under the mis - tle - toe _____ with you, _____ shaw - ty, with you, _

_____ with you, _____ shaw - ty, with you, _____ with you, _____

_____ un - der the mis - tle - toe. _____

_____ Kiss me un - der - neath the mis - tle - toe. _____

Show me, ba - by, that you love me so, oh oh, _____

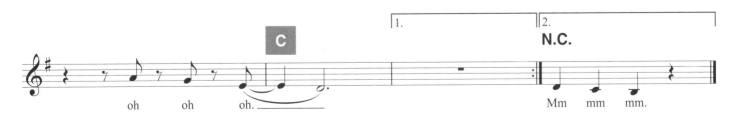

oh oh oh. _____ Mm mm mm.

Not That Far from Bethlehem

Words and Music by Jeff Borders, Gayla Borders and Lowell Alexander

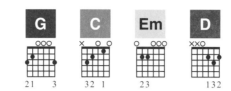

Verse
Slowly

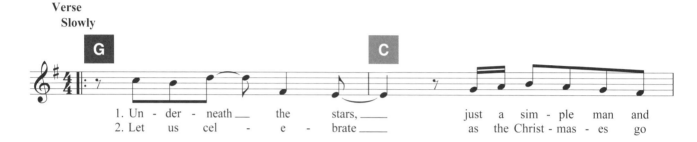

1. Un - der - neath ___ the stars, ___ just a sim - ple man and
2. Let us cel - e - brate ___ as the Christ - mas - es go

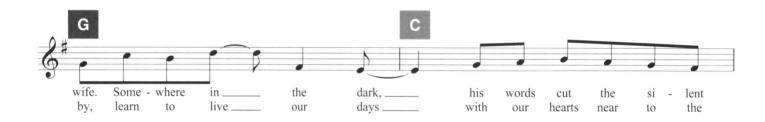

wife. Some - where in ___ the dark, ___ his words cut the si - lent
by, learn to live ___ our days ___ with our hearts near to the

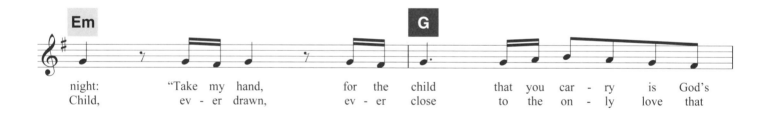

night: "Take my hand, for the child that you car - ry is God's
Child, ev - er drawn, for ev - er close to the on - ly love that

own. ___ And though it seems the ___
lasts. ___ And though two thou - sand ___

road is long, ___ we're not that far ___ from Beth - le - hem, _____ where
years have passed, _ we're not that far ___ from Beth - le - hem, _____ where

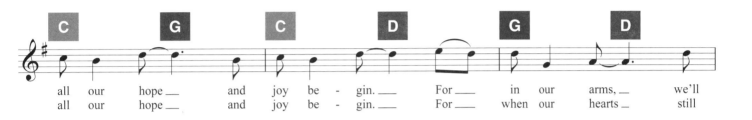

all our hope ___ and joy be - gin. ___ For ___ in our arms, ___ we'll
all our hope ___ and joy be - gin. ___ For ___ when our hearts _ still

cher - ish Him. _____ We're not that far _____
cher - ish Him, _____ we're not that far

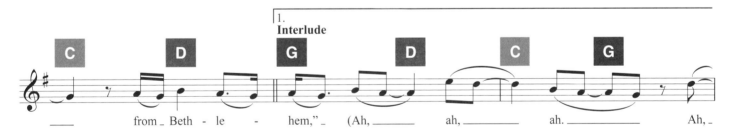

1.
Interlude

___ from _ Beth - le - hem," _ (Ah, _____ ah, _____ ah. _____ Ah,

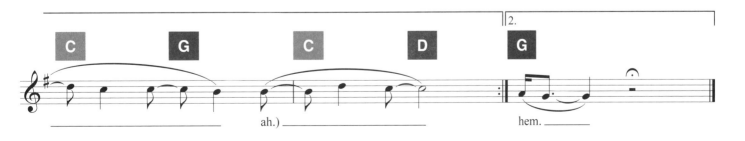

2.

_____ ah.) _____ hem. _____

Nuttin' for Christmas

Words and Music by Roy Bennett and Sid Tepper

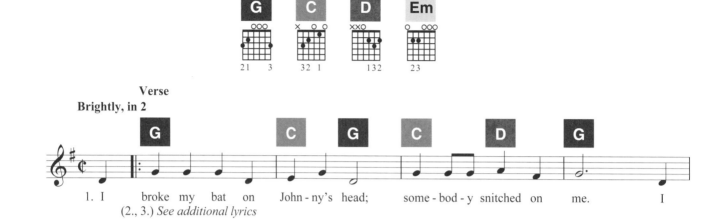

Verse
Brightly, in 2

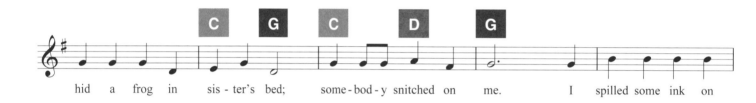

1. I broke my bat on John-ny's head; some-bod-y snitched on me. I
(2., 3.) *See additional lyrics*

hid a frog in sis-ter's bed; some-bod-y snitched on me. I spilled some ink on

Mom-my's rug, I made Tom-my eat a bug, bought some gum with a pen-ny slug;

Chorus

some-bod-y snitched on me. Oh, I'm get-tin' nut-tin' for Christ-mas.

Mom-my and Dad-dy are mad.

I'm get-tin' nut-tin' for Christ-mas, 'cause

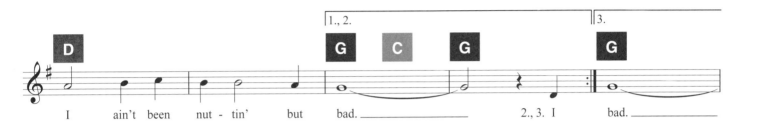

I ain't been nut-tin' but bad. _____ 2., 3. I bad. _____

Outro

_____ So you bet-ter be good, what-ev-er you do, 'cause if you're bad, I'm

warn-ing you: you'll get nut-tin' for Christ-mas. _____

Additional Lyrics

2. I put a tack on teacher's chair;
Somebody snitched on me.
I tied a knot in Susie's hair;
Somebody snitched on me.
I did a dance on Mommy's plants,
Climbed a tree and tore my pants.
Filled the sugar bowl with ants;
Somebody snitched on me.

3. I won't be seeing Santa Claus;
Somebody snitched on me.
He won't come visit me because
Somebody snitched on me.
Next year, I'll be going straight.
Next year, I'll be good, just wait.
I'd start now, but it's too late;
Somebody snitched on me.

O Come, Little Children

Words by C. von Schmidt
Music J.P.A. Schulz

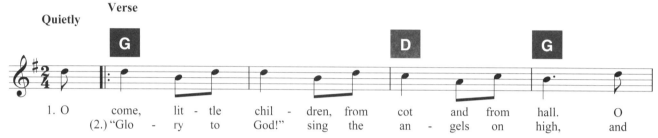

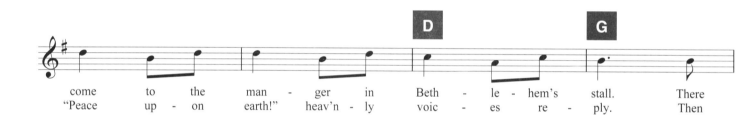

O Come, O Come, Emmanuel

Traditional Latin Text
15th Century French Melody

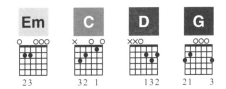

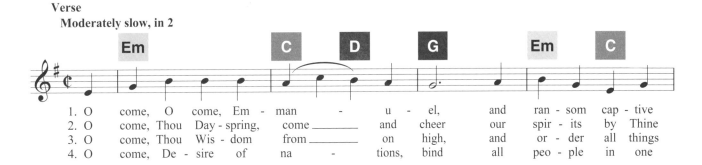

1. O come, O come, Em - man - u - el, and ran - som cap - tive
2. O come, Thou Day - spring, come _____ and cheer our spir - its by Thine
3. O come, Thou Wis - dom from _____ on high, and or - der all things
4. O come, De - sire of na - tions, bind all peo - ple in one

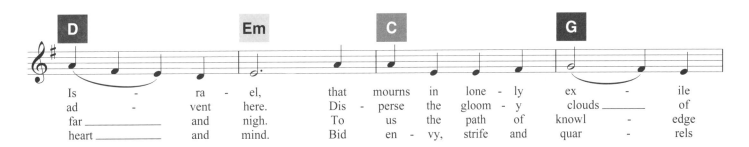

Is - ra - el, that mourns in lone - ly ex - ile
ad - vent here. Dis - perse the gloom - y clouds _____ of
far _____ and nigh. To us the path of knowl - edge
heart _____ and mind. Bid en - vy, strife and quar - rels

here un - til the Son of God _____ ap - pear.
night, and death's dark shad - ows put _____ to flight.
show, and cause us in her ways _____ to go.
cease; fill the whole world with heav - en's peace. } Re -

Chorus

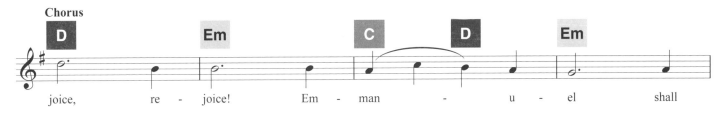

joice, re - joice! Em - man - u - el shall

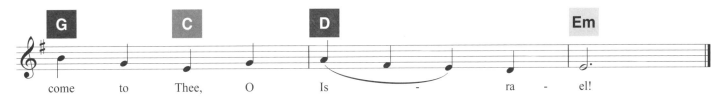

come to Thee, O Is - ra - el!

Old Toy Trains

Words and Music by Roger Miller

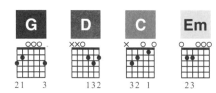

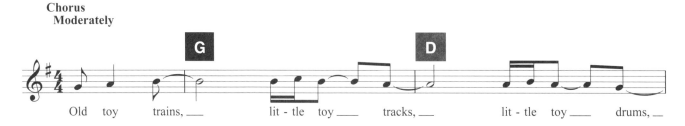

Chorus
Moderately

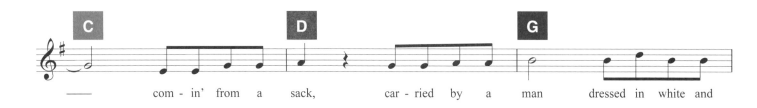

Old toy trains, ___ lit - tle toy ___ tracks, ___ lit - tle toy ___ drums, ___

___ com - in' from a sack, car - ried by a man dressed in white and

red. Lit - tle boy, ___ don't ___ you think it's time you were in bed? Close your

Bridge

eyes, ___ lis - ten to the skies. ___

___ All is calm, all is well; soon you'll hear Kris

Krin - gle and the jin - gle ___ bell bring - in' lit - tle toy ___ trains, ___ lit - tle toy ___ tracks, ___

___ lit - tle toy ___ drums ___ com - in' from a sack, car - ried by a

man dressed in white and red. Lit - tle boy, ___ don't ___ you think it's time you were in

bed? So close your bed? Lit - tle boy, ___ don't ___

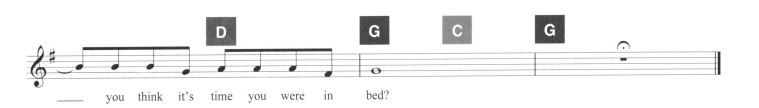

___ you think it's time you were in bed?

Once in Royal David's City

Words by Cecil F. Alexander
Music by Henry J. Gauntlett

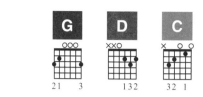

Verse
Moderately

1. Once in roy - al Da - vid's __ cit - y stood a low - ly cat - tle __ shed,
2.–4. *See additional lyrics*

where a moth - er laid __ her __ ba - by in a man - ger for __ His __ bed.

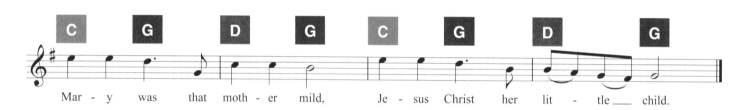

Mar - y was that moth - er mild, Je - sus Christ her lit - tle __ child.

Additional Lyrics

2. He came down to earth from heaven,
Who is God and Lord of all,
And His shelter was a stable,
And His cradle was a stall:
With the poor, and mean, and lowly,
Lived on earth our Savior holy.

3. Jesus is our childhood's pattern,
Day by day like us He grew;
He was little, weak and helpless,
Tears and smiles like us He knew:
And He feeleth for our sadness,
And He shareth in our gladness.

4. And our eyes at last shall see Him,
Through his own redeeming love.
For the child so dear and gentle
Is our Lord in heav'n above.
And He leads His children on
To the place where He is gone.

One for the Little Bitty Baby
(Go Where I Send Thee)

Spiritual Arranged by Ronnie Gilbert, Lee Hays, Fred Hellerman and Pete Seeger

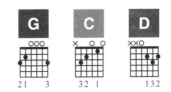

Verse
Spirited, in 2

Chil - dren, go where I send thee! How shall I send thee?

(Repeat from 2nd verse on, reading up, until all previous verses have been sung)

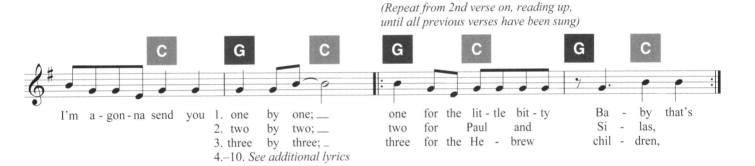

I'm a-gon-na send you 1. one by one; ___ one for the lit-tle bit-ty Ba - by that's
2. two by two; ___ two for Paul and Si - las,
3. three by three; ___ three for the He - brew chil - dren,
4.–10. *See additional lyrics*

born, born, ___ born in Beth - le - hem.

Additional Lyrics

4. I'm a-gonna send you four by four;
   Four for the four that stood at the door,

5. I'm a-gonna send you five by five;
   Five for the gospel preachers,

6. I'm a-gonna send you six by six;
   Six for the six that never got fixed,

7. I'm a-gonna send you seven by seven;
   Seven for the seven that never got to heaven,

8. I'm a-gonna send you eight by eight;
   Eight for the eight that stood at the gate,

9. I'm a-gonna send you nine by nine;
   Nine for the nine all dressed so fine,

10. I'm a-gonna send you ten by ten;
    Ten for the ten commandments,

Pretty Paper

Words and Music by Willie Nelson

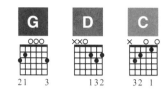

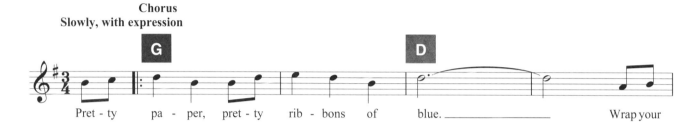

Chorus
Slowly, with expression

Pret - ty pa - per, pret - ty rib - bons of blue. Wrap your

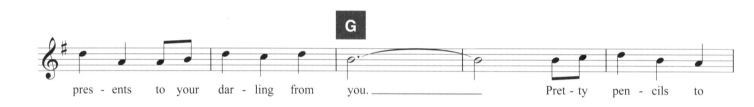

pres - ents to your dar - ling from you. Pret - ty pen - cils to

write, "I love you." Pret - ty pa - per, pret - ty

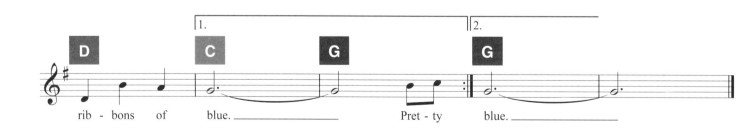

rib - bons of blue. Pret - ty blue.

Silent Night

Words by Joseph Mohr
Translated by John F. Young
Music by Franz X. Gruber

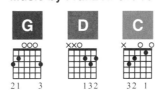

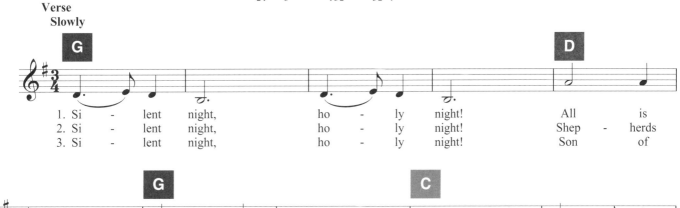

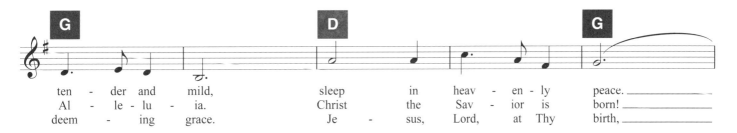

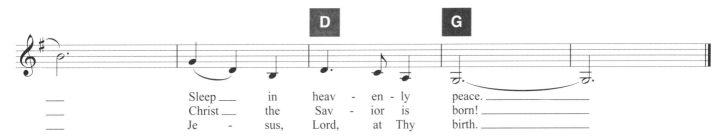

Shake Me I Rattle
(Squeeze Me I Cry)

Words and Music by Hal Hackady and Charles Naylor

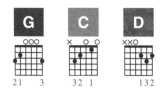

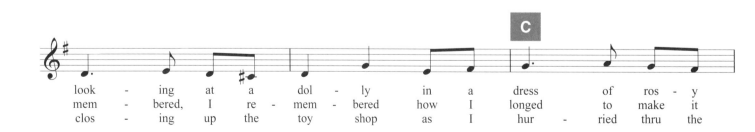

red,   and   a - round   the   pret - ty   dol - ly   hung   a
mine,   and   a - round   that   oth - er   dol - ly   hung   an -
door,   just   in   time   to   buy   the   dol - ly   that   her

lit - tle   sign   that   said: Shake   me,   I
oth - er   lit - tle   sign: Shake   me,   I   I
heart   was   long - ing   for.   Shake   me,   I

rat - tle.   Squeeze   me,   I   cry.   As   I
rat - tle.   Squeeze   me,   I   cry.   I   had
rat - tle.   Squeeze   me,   I   cry.   And   I

stood   there   be - side   her,   I   could   hear   her
count - ed   be   my   pen - nies,   just   a   pen - ny
gave   her   the   dol - ly   that   we   both   had   longed   to

sigh.)
shy. }   Shake   me,   I   rat - tle.
buy.)

Squeeze   me,   I   cry.   Please   take   me   home   and

love ___ me. ___   2. I   re - ___
                        3. It   was

71

Silver Bells

from the Paramount Picture THE LEMON DROP KID
Words and Music by Jay Livingston and Ray Evans

1. Cit - y side - walks, bus - y side - walks dressed in hol - i - day style, in the
(2.) street - lights, e - ven stop - lights blink a bright red and green, as the

air there's a feel - ing of Christ - mas. Chil - dren laugh - ing, peo - ple
shop - pers rush home with their treas - ures. Hear the snow crunch, see the

pass - ing, meet - ing smile af - ter smile, and on ev - 'ry street cor - ner you'll
kids bunch, this is San - ta's big scene, and a - bove all this bus - tle you'll

Chorus

hear: _____ Sil - ver bells, _____ sil - ver bells. _____
hear: _____

_____ It's Christ - mas time in the cit - y.

Ring - a - ling, _____ hear them ring. _____ Soon it will

1.
be Christ - mas day. 2. Strings of

2.
day.

Up on the Housetop

Words and Music by B.R. Hanby

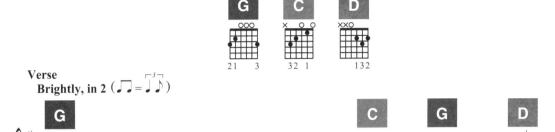

Verse
Brightly, in 2

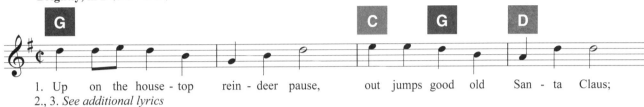

1. Up on the house-top rein-deer pause, out jumps good old San-ta Claus;
2., 3. *See additional lyrics*

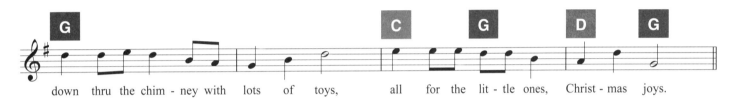

down thru the chim-ney with lots of toys, all for the lit-tle ones, Christ-mas joys.

Chorus

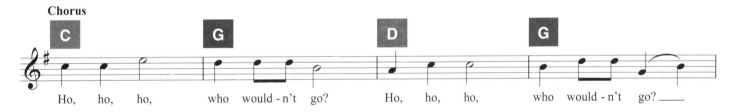

Ho, ho, ho, who would-n't go? Ho, ho, ho, who would-n't go? ____

Up on the house-top, click, click, click. Down through the chim-ney with good Saint Nick.

Additional Lyrics

2. First comes the stocking of Little Nell.
Oh, dear Santa, fill it well.
Give her a dollie that laughs and cries,
One that will open and shut her eyes.

3. Next comes the stocking of little Will.
Oh, just see what a glorious fill!
Here is a hammer and lots of tacks,
Also a ball and a whip that cracks.

The Star Carol
(Canzone d'i Zampognari)

English Lyric and Music Adaptation by Peter Seeger
(Based on a Traditional Neapolitan Carol)

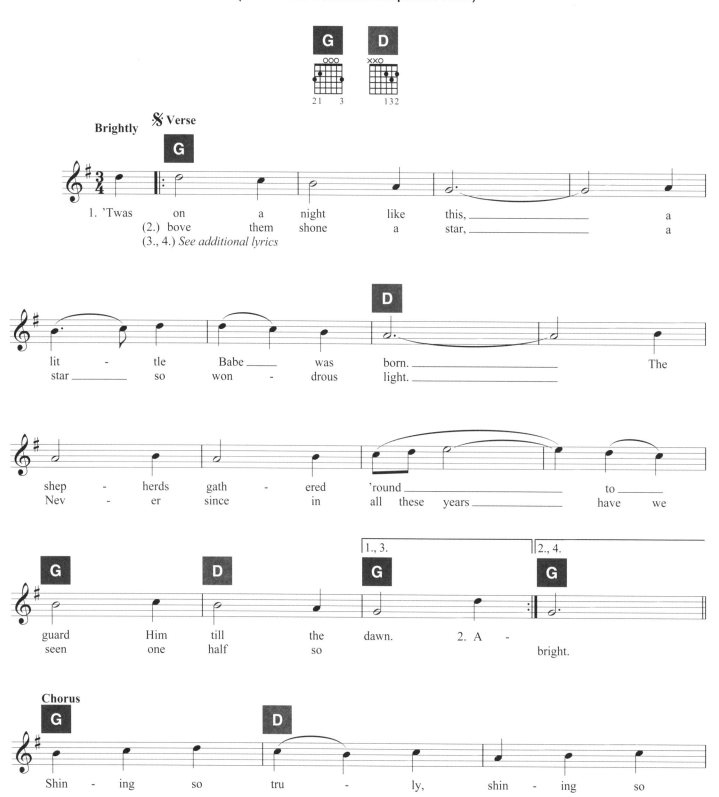

Brightly **Verse**

1. 'Twas on a night like this, _____ a a
(2.) bove them shone a star, _____ a
(3., 4.) *See additional lyrics*

lit - tle Babe ___ was born. _____ The
star ___ so won - drous light. _____

shep - herds gath - ered 'round _____ to ___
Nev - er since in all these years _____ have we

1., 3.
2., 4.

guard Him till the dawn. 2. A -
seen one till half so bright.

Chorus

Shin - ing so tru - ly, shin - ing so

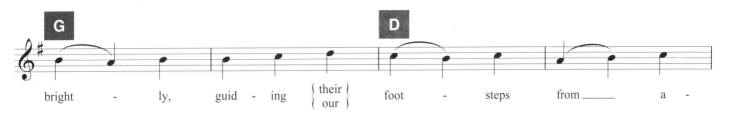

bright - ly, guid - ing { their / our } foot - steps from _____ a -

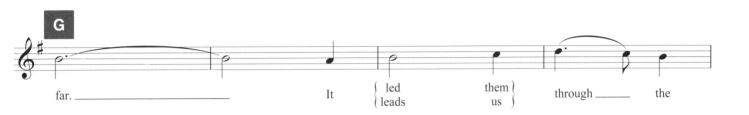

far. _____ It { led them / leads us } through _____ the

night, _____ a path to love and

broth - er - hood, _____ by _____ fol - low - ing its

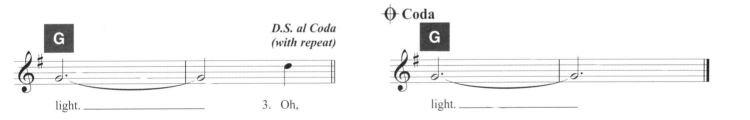

light. _____ 3. Oh,

light. _____

Additional Lyrics

3. Oh, come with us tonight
   And join us on our way,
   For we have found that star once more
   To greet a better day.

4. For though throughout our land
   Men search the skies in vain,
   Yet turn their glance within their hearts,
   They would find this star again.

What a Merry Christmas This Could Be

Words and Music by Hank Cochran and Harlan Howard

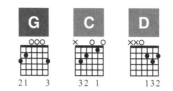

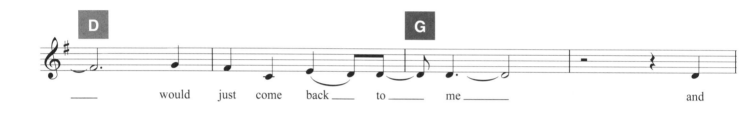

What a mer - ry Christ - mas this could be if you would just come back to me and

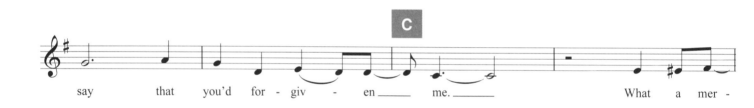

say that you'd for - giv - en me. What a mer -

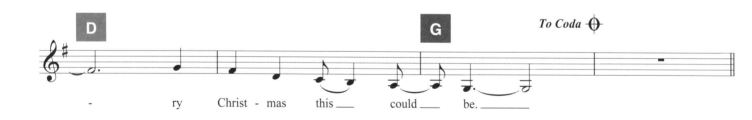

- ry Christ - mas this could be.

It was just last Christ - mas that we quar - reled and you walked out.

I knew ___ I was wrong, ___ but you'd ___ come

back; I ___ had no doubt. Now a year ___ has rolled a - round; ___ it's

Christ - mas once a - gain, and what I'd give if

D.S. al Coda

Coda

you'd ___ come ___ walk - in' ___ in. What a mer - What a mer -

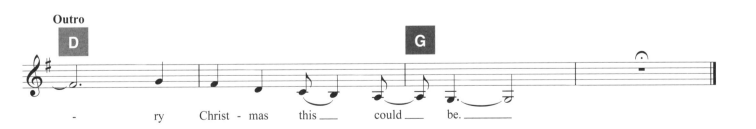

Outro

- ry Christ - mas this ___ could ___ be. ___

Where Are You Christmas?

from DR. SEUSS' HOW THE GRINCH STOLE CHRISTMAS

Words and Music by Will Jennings, James Horner and Mariah Carey

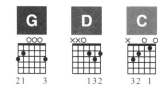

1. Where are you, Christ - mas? Why can't I find you?
4. I feel you, Christ - mas. I know I found you.

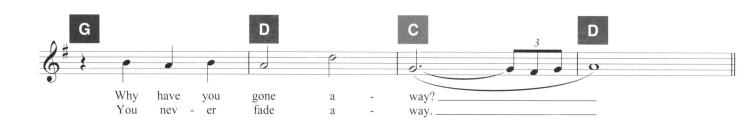

Why have you gone a - way? _____
You nev - er fade a - way. _____

2. Where is the laugh - ter you used to bring me?
3. Where are you, Christ - mas? Do you re - mem - ber
5. The joy of Christ - mas stays here in - side us,

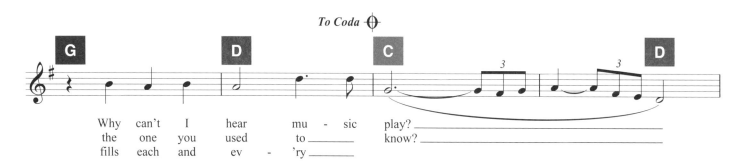

Why can't I hear mu - sic play? _____
the one you used to _____ know? _____
fills each and ev - 'ry _____

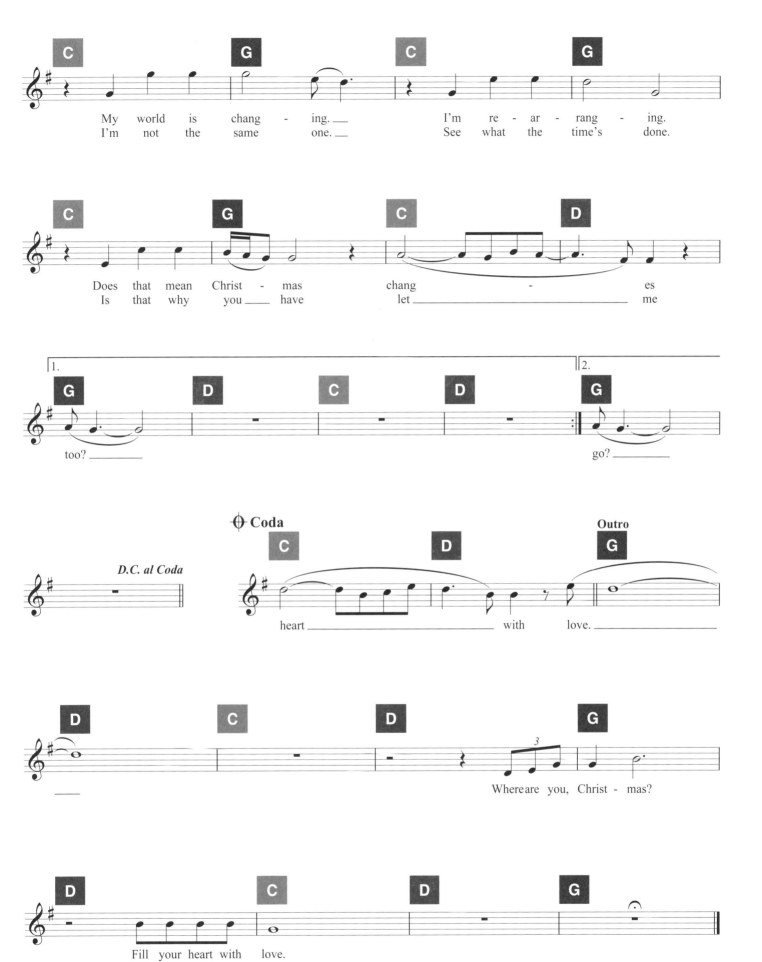

While Shepherds Watched Their Flocks

Words by Nahum Tate
Music by George Frideric Handel

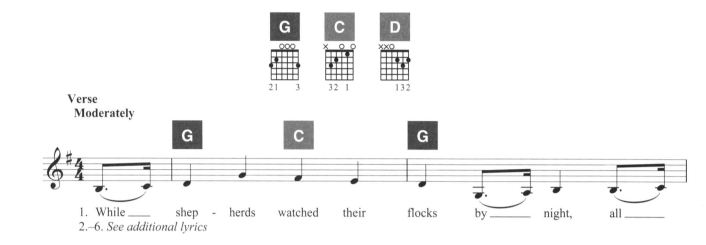

Verse
Moderately

1. While ___ shep - herds watched their flocks by ___ night, all ___
2.–6. *See additional lyrics*

seat - ed on the ___ ground, _ the ___ an - gel of the Lord came _ down and ___

glo - ry shone a - round, ___ and glo - ry shone a - round.

Additional Lyrics

2. "Fear not!" said he, for mighty dread
   Had seized their troubled mind.
   "Glad tidings of great joy I bring
   To you and all mankind,
   To you and all mankind.

3. "To you, in David's town this day,
   Is born of David's line,
   The Savior, who is Christ the Lord;
   And this shall be the sign,
   And this shall be the sign:

4. "The heav'nly Babe you there shall find
   To human view displayed,
   All meanly wrapped in swathing bands
   And in a manger laid,
   And in a manger laid."

5. Thus spake the seraph, and forthwith
   Appeared a shining throng
   Of angels praising God on high,
   Who thus addressed their song,
   Who thus addressed their song:

6. "All glory be to God on high,
   And to the earth be peace.
   Good will henceforth from heav'n to men,
   Begin and never cease,
   Begin and never cease!"